# 1 MONTH OF
# FREE
## READING

at

## www.ForgottenBooks.com

By purchasing this book you are eligible for one month membership to ForgottenBooks.com, giving you unlimited access to our entire collection of over 1,000,000 titles via our web site and mobile apps.

To claim your free month visit:

www.forgottenbooks.com/free890755

ISBN 978-0-266-79636-7
PIBN 10890755

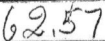

# THE
# WORLD'S BEST DAHLIAS

## NEW CREATIONS AND OLD FRIENDS

QUEEN
Elizabeth
SEE
DESCRIPTION
ON PAGE 1

ACTUAL SIZE
7 ½ IN'S

# PEACOCK DAHLIA FARMS

FARMS
WILLIAMSTOWN JUNCTION
NEW JERSEY

MAIL ADDRESS
BERLIN POST OFFICE
NEW JERSEY

*"Mecca" of Dahlia Lovers. More than 10,000 visitors weekly at the World's Largest Dahlia Farm*

**A**GAIN we come to you, with thanks for your generous patronage in the past, and assurance that we will give as near 100 per cent. efficiency as is possible in the future. On the following pages will be found THE PLAIN TRUTH, about THE WORLD'S BEST DAHLIAS. Large, very large, medium or small, together with color, form, or other characteristics, as we see it here, will be set forth.

We are glad to note the craze for size alone has about run out. A Dahlia now must have more than size to commend it. Of course we all like to exhibit a flower larger than ever before shown, but, nothing can take the place of those brilliantly colored beauties, or those exquisitely formed, delicately tinted, medium or even small sized flowers, with good stiff slender stems, that lend themselves most admirably to all kinds of decorations—garden, home, hall, business establishment or personal adornment. For after all it is only natural to love the beautiful and artistic, rather than the Bizarre. We may like the elephant, but we love the horse.

THE PEACOCK DAHLIA FARMS ARE THE LARGEST IN THE WORLD and have the largest and best equipped warehouse and storage cellar, a section of which is shown above. It contains 11,288 sq. ft. of floor space and 125,420 cubic feet of space. It is built of concrete, with an electric light plant attached, and a heating plant located 75 ft. away.

**OUR MAIN FARMS** are located at Williamstown Junction, on the Atlantic City branch of the Reading R. R., Ferry foot of Chestnut Street, Philadelphia, also one mile south of the famous White Horse Pike from Philadelphia to Atlantic City, also 2½ miles by direct road from Berlin.

We cordially invite all to visit and see for themselves the LARGEST DAHLIA FARMS IN THE WORLD—THE HOUSE OF THE WORLD'S BEST DAHLIA.

**ORDER EARLY** It will greatly facilitate shipments if orders are sent in early. We aim to send out orders the same or the next day after receipt, but during the rush season this is impossible—hence the advisability of ordering early.

---

**Guarantee.** We guarantee every plant, bulb or root sent out by us to be just as represented, absolutely true to name, reach destination safely in perfect condition, and prove entirely satisfactory; we will cheerfully replace any that should prove otherwise.

**Terms.** Cash with order. Remittances may be made by Bank Draft, Post Office or Express Money Order, or Registered Letter at our expense and our risk.

**Forwarding.** Dahlia Roots and Plants are sent by mail postpaid at prices named herein; but larger stock will be sent by express, charges collect, and "Extras" are added to help cover charges. Dahlias are billed at "2nd class" rates and in most cases are one-third (⅓) or 33⅓ per cent. less than regular merchandise rates.

**Errors.** While we exercise every care, errors may occur occasionally. In such a case kindly notify us at once, and correction will be promptly and cheerfully made.

**Name and Address.** Be sure and write name and address plainly on each order or communication.

Address all orders or communications to

**PEACOCK DAHLIA FARMS,**

**Berlin Post Office, N. J.**

| MODEL | PERLEHILDE | MRS. WINSTANLEY | DUCHESS OF MARLBORO |

*View of a field of Cactus Dahlias*

# DAHLIAS FOR 1921

Once more we have added many new and improved varieties to our list, but have discarded still more, keeping in this way always our high standard—THE WORLD'S BEST DAHLIAS.

## Classification and Culture

We will send free on request our pamphlet on culture and classification.

## New Book "The Dahlia"—Fifth Edition

By Lawrence K. Peacock, 80 pages, 7¾ by 10¾, beautifully illustrated. Fifth and revised edition. A practical treatise on its habits, characteristics, culture and history by one who for 36 years has never failed to have a crop of the finest blooms, in their season regardless of conditions. Price, 50c. postpaid. FREE on request with all orders amounting to $5.00 or more.

**QUEEN ELIZABETH** This new Paeony Dahlia shown in color on the front cover page is the highest type yet produced in this class. Note the wonderful formation of the curled center petals, which completely cover the center. This illustration is reproduced from a photograph of a flower over 7 inches across. The color is a beautiful rosy mauve. The large flowers are facing, on very long (2½ to 4 ft.) stems, slender, yet stiff, holding the flowers erect. The plant is a very clean, strong grower and free bloomer, every shoot produces a flower. It is a variety that just will bloom. A flower that should be in every collection. Valuable for cutting, exhibition and the garden. Roots, $1.00 each.

**GOLDEN WEST CACTUS** See color illustration on last cover page, reproduced from a photograph. This is a California variety that is **in a class by itself**, in its color— that **rich golden, bronzy yellow, with** the **scarlet shading** at the base of the petals and the center. It is a wonderful grower, strong and sturdy, with heavy, clean healthy leaves, and branching habit, producing the large flowers freely on long stiff stems. The flower is large, 6 to 8 inches across, the outer petals reflexing somewhat, and a full high center, making it very deep. It is the greatest seller as a cut flower, a winner for exhibition and a wonder as a garden plant. Should be in every collection. Price, roots, $1.00 each.

**SPECIAL OFFER.** We will send one root each of **Queen Elizabeth** and **Golden West Cactus**, prepaid for $1.75.

# NEW INTRODUCTIONS OF 1921

**CHARLES LAWRENCE** One of our new Florida productions, No. D. 2. This is the immense rich crimson decorative that attracted so much attention the past two years, at our farms, and at our exhibitions, at Wanamaker's, in Philadelphia. Color, full crimson, richly shaded. Size, 7 to 8 inches across and 3 to 4 inches deep; of great substance and a good keeper. It is of splendid form, with full high center, and as it develops, the outer petals reflex to the stem.

A wonderfully strong, vigorous grower, of branching habit, with dark glossy green foliage, showing its rugged constitution. The giant flowers are produced, freely and continuously, on long erect stems, with the flowers facing boldly. Height, 5 feet. Stock limited. Strong roots, $10.00 each.

**MARY STEFFENSON** This is F, 1941, and another of our Florida productions, that has elicited the most profuse admiration and praise. A new creation in form and coloring—nothing like it—even the buds are distinctive, being very long, slender and pointed, with a cluster of long green bract to protect them. It is a cross of Fantasie (offered by some as Mme. Butterfly) and Mrs. J. Harrison Dick. With its free blooming, on long slender, but stiff, yet graceful, stems, it is, without doubt, the most delicately lovely dahlia grown today.

We give the description, written by one of the most critical dahlia experts:—"Color, at base, citron yellow; outer half creamy white; both yellow and white mottled and overspread with rosolane pink. Many petals showing faint yellow along mid-veins. All dusted over with tiny glistening crystal-like particles as of gilt. Form full and graceful, something like Bertha von Suttner. Size, 5½ x 2¼. Petals recurved, acuminate, none cleft. Edges generally rolled in slightly. Many tips twisted and whorled. Bloom, facing on cane stiff stems, well above foliage. One of the best of them all." Height, 5 feet. Stock limited. Roots, $10.00 each.

**PATRICK O'MARA** This sensational new decorative variety was awarded a Gold Medal by the American Dahlia Society, as the best Autumn shade variety in existence. The color is an unusually soft and pleasing shade of orange-buff, slightly tinged with Neyron rose. It is very large, 7 to 9 inches in diameter, and borne on long strong erect stems. It is a strong vigorous grower and free bloomer. The giant flowers are well formed, with good full center, while the outer petals are most pleasingly irregular. Strong plants, spring delivery, $10.00 each.

**JAMES WELLER** (Century). The finest of all single Dahlias, of largest size and the most beautiful color combination—a rich golden yellow, with one-third of each petal overlaid soft rosy red. The two colors blend most harmoniously and are very effective. The big flowers are produced freely on long stiff stems, and are remarkable good keepers. This variety is most striking and effective, and is one of natures masterpieces. Height, 5 feet. Strong roots, $2.00.

**KATHERINE DE LA MARE** (Decorative). A new variety we have been growing for commercial cut flowers, and are now offering for the first time. Color is clear yellow at base of petal, passing to primrose, overlaid and suffused pink, shading to rose at the tips of the outer petals. The flowers are of beautiful form and quite large, about 6 to 8 inches, and are produced on long erect stems, facing. A strong vigorous, branching, upright grower. A fine all-around exhibition, cut flower and garden variety that we cannot recommend too highly. Height, 4 feet. Roots, $2.00 each.

**KITTY DE LA MARE** (Decorative). One of, if not the most profuse blooming of the class. A cross between Katherine De La Mare and a primrose seedling. It is similar to the above, but medium in size (4 to 5 inches) and always full to the center. It is a very strong, vigorous grower, very branching habit, producing flowers of medium size and lovely pink tinged pink color on long stiff stems in the greatest profusion. For all kinds of cut flower work or for the garden it cannot be excelled. It is undoubtedly the finest growing plant we have ever seen and will produce more perfect long stemmed flowers during the season than any other Dahlia. Height, 5 feet. Roots, $2.00 each.

**NANCY ALDEN** (Decorative). Raised by and named after a direct descendent of John Alden, and is characteristic of the puritan maiden; light pink, suffused deep pink. The pink shades are clear and the flowers are held erect on long stems. A remarkably free bloomer and one of the very earliest to bloom. It has been grown exclusively for cut flowers for several years, and is now being offered for the first time. Height, 4 feet. Roots, $1.00 each.

**ROBERT SHEPPARD** (Decorative). This is our D. 1, that has been admired so much for its many all-around good qualities. Color is ruby red, shaded and suffused maroon—a color entirely distinct. Flowers are large, 7 inches and more across, produced freely on long graceful stems. It is an early and continuous bloomer. Height, 5 feet. Roots, $2.00 each.

**SEMINOLE** (Decorative). F. 1932, under which number it was greatly admired the past season. Color is a soft dark velvety cardinal, one of the richest shades, and is covered with a glistening sheen. Flowers of fine form, full center and outer petals reflex, inner petals are slightly rolled in, pointed, some are twisted and whorled. A fine growing plant and a profuse bloomer, facing, on cane stiff stems, held well above the foliage. Height, 3½ feet. Roots, $2.00 each.

**TYRREL AUSTIN** (Paeony). This giant new variety is a seedling of the well-known F. R. Austin, but is entirely distinct, being larger, entirely distinct in color and formation. Size 7 to 9 inches. Color, outer petals a rich carmine red, inner petals are beautifully blended and veined carmine, shades of yellow and pink. The petals are twisted and whorled in a most pleasing manner. An early and profuse bloomer and strong vigorous grower. A great acquisition. Height, 5 feet. Roots, $3.00.

**SPECIAL OFFER.** One each of the preceding 10 wonderful new Dahlias now offered for the first time, by parcel post, prepaid, for $40.00.

*Gladys Sherwood is undoubtedly the largest white Cactus Dahlia in existence. Now offered for first time at $5.00 each*

*Hybrid Cactus Dahlia, "BIANCA." (See description below)*

# New and Rare Cactus Dahlias

This collection embraces the World's Best Cactus Dahlias. Not only the largest size but all types and good growers and bloomers. Our stock is not only true to name but true to type.

**BIANCA.** A magnificent new hybrid cactus that is in a class by itself, of giant size and splendid form. (See illustration.) The color is white, suffused and overlaid an exquisite soft mauve pink. A strong vigorous grower of splendid habits and a very free bloomer. The gigantic flowers are facing and held erect on long stiff stems..... $1.00

**BLENDA.** Rich crimson, shaded maroon, pinkish white at base of petals. Flowers are large with long narrow incurved petals. A strikingly handsome flower that should be in every collection.................................. .50

**Bridal Robe.** One of the very best white cactus for all purposes. Flowers are very large, of great substance and keeping qualities. They are produced on long stiff but graceful stems. Flowers are from 6 to 8 inches across with great depth. A strong vigorous grower and continuous bloomer.......................................... .50

**CREPUSCLE.** Yellow, shaded deep orange. The flowers are very large, of good form and a very profuse bloomer for so large a flower. The plant is a strong vigorous grower of medium height and a very reliable and continuous bloomer.............................................. .50

**CRYSTAL.** One of the very finest, clear soft pink cactus. Flowers are of large size with long narrow incurved petals and full centres. A strong vigorous grower and profuse bloomer. An excellent variety for exhibition and garden. (See illustration, page 4)............................. $0.75

**Dolly.** A very distinct and striking variety. Color rich crimson scarlet, tipped pure white. A combination that always attracts attention. The petals are long, narrow and incurved. The best of its type................. .50

**Dorothy Hawes.** Large clear rosy purple with long narrow incurved petals. The plant is a strong vigorous grower, producing the flowers freely on long graceful stems..... .30

**DUCHESS OF MARLBORO.** A magnificent cactus, most pleasing and effective; rich golden orange, overlaid solferino. The flowers are of splendid form with long, narrow twisted incurved petals; large size and produced freely on long graceful stems........................... .50

**EDITH CARTER.** A soft bright yellow, suffused and heavily tipped bright rosy carmine. Of fine form, good size and produced freely on long stiff stems. An unusually lovely variety. The plant is an early, free and continuous bloomer............................................ .75

*Queen Elizabeth and Golden West Cactus, our two colored cover Dahlias, best of their class, for $1.75*

*Cactus Dahlia, "CRYSTAL."*  (*See description, page 3*)

**ELECTRIC.**  This is one of the most charming varieties. The color is rich clear canary yellow, each petal heavily tipped white; delicate and chaste. The flowers are large and finely formed with incurved petals................ Each $0.50

**Excelsior.**  A splendid garden and exhibition variety, color rich velvety maroon................................. .50

**FLORID.**  Bright scarlet, beautiful flowers with long narrow petals; borne on long stems................. .50

**FRANCIS WHITE.**  A splendid new white cactus of exquisite form with long narrow incurved and twisted petals. Large size, 5 to 7 inches across, borne on long graceful stems. Color pure white shading to sulphur at centre. An early and extremely profuse bloomer. One of the best for garden and exhibition................ .50

**F. W. FELLOWS.**  Flowers of immense size. Composed of numerous long narrow incurved petals of a lively orange scarlet. This is one of the largest and finest Autumn shade varieties. Should be in every collection........ 1.00

**GENERAL PERSHING.**  A very large creamy white hybrid cactus, with curved and twisted petals. A strong vigorous grower and profuse bloomer. Color white with cream shadings at centre........................ .75

**GLADYS SHERWOOD.**  The giant California white Hybrid Cactus. This is one of, if not the largest white cactus in existence. Flowers are 8 to 10 inches across with a possibility of 12 inches under high cultivation and disbudded. The plant is a remarkably fine grower of medium height, branching habit, and a free bloomer. The petals are very long, somewhat twisted and curled. Offered now for the first time at.................... 5.00

**GOLDEN EAGLE.**  Very large, bright yellow suffused rose fawn. The petals are long, narrow and pointed. Produced on extremely long graceful stems. A profuse bloomer........................................ Each $0.50

**GOLDEN WEST CACTUS.**  See description, page 1... 1.00

**H. H. Thomas.**  One of the finest forms of the incurved cactus type. Flowers are very large with numerous long narrow incurved petals. A beautiful deep rich crimson. A strong vigorous grower. One of the best exhibition varieties........................................ .75

**Indomitable.**  A very fine lilac mauve with lighter tips. A strong grower, early and continuous bloomer........ .50

**Jenny Wren.**  A fine shade of yellow, suffused and overlaid pink. An excellent exhibition variety........... .50

**Jupiter.**  A magnificent exhibition variety of immense size and an early and continuous bloomery The color is a bronzy buff, penciled and striped deep crimson. Occasionally the flowers are solid crimson. The best of this type........................................ .50

**Marguerite Bouchon.**  A magnificent large full flower. Centre pure white, outer petals a brilliant yet soft violet rose tipped white. A strong grower producing the flowers freely on long rigid yet graceful stems.............. .75

**MELODY CACTUS.**  An immense flower with very long, narrow twisted and incurved petals. The color is most beautiful and striking. Clear yellow at the base, heavily tipped white. A color combination that appeals to all. Occasionally the flowers are solid yellow. A magnificent exhibition variety................................ .75

*Mary Steffenson is the most delicately lovely, artistically formed and gracefully carried, a winner, $10.00*

4

**Milton Howard.** A most pleasing and distinct new Cactus Dahlia that appeals to all. Color clear pink, tipped white. A fine exhibition variety...................... $0.50

**Miss London.** A very large and beautifully blended exhibition cactus. Color deep rose tinged yellow.......... .50

**Miss Stredwick.** A very fine English Cactus of large size with very long narrow pointed petals. The plant is a fine grower, producing the flowers on long slender stems. Beautiful rose pink with creamy white centre.......... .25

**MME. ESCHENAUER.** An ideal Dahlia of exceptional merit. Most pleasing and effective color, being yellow at base of petals, passing to creamy white, suffused and tipped pale lilac. Delicate and chaste................. .75

**Mme. Henri Cayeux.** Clear pink, tinting to white at the tips. Long slender petals. A strong grower and extremely profuse bloomer. We consider this an improvement on Marguerite Bouchon in that it is a stronger grower, more profuse bloomer and produces the flowers on long straight stems...................... .75

**MODEL.** A beautiful cactus of exquisite form and coloring, being a clear yellow, passing to rose; very distinct and effective. A strong grower and an early, free and profuse bloomer................................ .75

**MRS. C. G. WYATT.** A beautiful pure white cactus of large size with long narrow incurved petals. An early, profuse and continuous bloomer on long stiff stems.... .50

**MRS. SEAL.** A very striking cactus that is greatly admired by many. The flowers are large, deep maroon, tipped light rose and white. The colors are so harmoniously blended and it is such a profuse bloomer that it will be a valuable acquisition to those that like variegated or multi-colored flowers......................... .35

**NANTWICH.** One of the very finest of the incurved petaled cactus. It is a strong vigorous grower of upright habit and the flowers are produced freely on good stiff stems. A beautiful golden orange shading deeper at the centre........................................ .50

**PIERROT.** Immense size with very long incurved petals; deep amber, distinctly tipped white, sometimes solid amber. A magnificent exhibition and garden variety. It is a very strong vigorous grower, producing the giant flowers profusely on very long slender graceful stems.. 1.00

**Primrose Queen.** A splendid flower with long narrow incurved petals. Clear primrose yellow. A very free bloomer.......................................... .50

**QUAKER CITY.** A fine new cactus of a most unique and attractive form. The flowers are large and each of the broad pointed petals is supplemented with 3 to 6 narrow pointed petals, giving it a most artistic effect. Color clear primrose yellow. A profuse bloomer............ 1.00

**RHEINISCHER FROHSINN.** One of the most strikingly attractive of all the cactus. Very large, with long pointed incurved petals. Color an iridescent crimson carmine tinting to white at the base of the petals. A good vigorous grower and bloomer. Producing the flowers on good stiff stems........................ 1.00

**Richard Box.** A superb yellow of large size and splendid form, with very long narrow pointed petals. Color, clear light yellow. An early and profuse bloomer...... .75

**SUCCESS.** One of the best for garden or exhibition. Clear yellow with long pointed petals; an early, free and continuous bloomer on long stems.................... .35

**SUNSET.** The best of the bronzy Autumn shades. Yellow at base, shading to bright apricot; full and free, with stiff stems. A fine garden and cut flower........ .50

**SWEET BRIAR.** One of the loveliest shades of clear soft pink; very long narrow incurved petals......... .75

**The Quaker.** A fine exhibition cactus, white suffused flesh pink, beautiful and chaste.................... .50

**Thos. Oberlin.** Very large fine flower, with long incurved petals. Color intense scarlet..................... .50

**WACHT AM RHINE.** Soft hydrangea pink, tinting to white at centre. A large striking flower with deeply cleft petals. A strong vigorous grower and profuse bloomer, on long slender stiff stems................ .75

**Special Offer—One root each of the above new and rare Cactus Dahlias. 44 varieties in all, by Parcel Post, prepaid, for $27.50.**

*Select Cactus Dahlia, "MARJORIE CASTLETON." (See description, page 6*

## Colossal Cactus Dahlias

These grand varieties are of giant size, having long rather broad petals, approaching the hybrid cactus in form.

**ATTRACTION.** Large, elegant flower of a clear lilac rose, borne on long stiff stems and a Dahlia of exceptional merit. A true paeony-cactus type................... $1.00

**COLOSSAL PEACE.** A massive cactus of the Kalif form and size, often measuring eight inches across. Later in the season when flower shows a centre it is a wonderful paeony Dahlia. Color creamy white at centre, shading violet rose with lighter tips. The plant is a very strong vigorous grower, of branching habit, an earl and profuse bloomer on long stems.............. y........ 2.00

**GEORGE WALTERS.** Not only one of the very best autumn shade varieties, but one of the best in existence. The flowers are of immense size with rather broad, heavy petals of great substance and good keeping qualities. The plant is a strong vigorous grower, producing the flowers on long stiff stems, making it fine for cut flowers and exhibition, as well as one of the best garden varieties. The color is a rich coppery old gold shading to buff at the centre. Should be in every collection............... 1.00

**GOLDEN GATE.** A large hybrid cactus of a rich deep golden yellow, suffused and shaded amber. Plant is a very heavy vigorous grower, producing the giant flowers on very long stiff but graceful stems.................. .50

**KALIF.** A very large pure scarlet red. A strong plant, producing the giant flowers freely on long stiff stems. This is undoubtedly the most popular red Cactus Dahlia today and one that gives universal satisfaction........ 1.00

**MRS. WARNAAR.** One of the best of the Holland productions. Of mammoth size, fine form and substance. Color, creamy white with apple blossom suffusion. An acquisition.................................... 1.50

**NIBELUNGENHORT.** Immense flowers 7 to 8 inches across, rich golden apricot, suffused old rose. The plant is also a giant, being very strong and vigorous, producing the massive flowers early and freely on very long stiff stems. It is entirely distinct, does well everywhere and should be in every garden collection. It is a fine exhibition variety.................................. 1.00

**WODAN.** Old gold at centre, shading to a salmon rose. This variety is in a class by itself, in-so-far as it is an extremely vigorous, almost rampant, grower, producing the big flowers profusely on very long stems. One of the best. .75

*If you want the BEST, you want Patrick O'Mara—the wonderful Autumn shade decorative*

**WOLFGANG VON GOETHE.** Large apricot, shaded Each carmine. An entirely distinct combination of colors and shades. The plant is an ideal grower of branching upright habit, a very profuse bloomer, producing the flowers on long stiff stems well above the foliage. One of the best for cutting and the garden................ $0.75

**YELLOW KING.** One of the largest of all cactus Dahlias, being of gigantic size and of the finest new cactus. Color light yellow, tinting to cream at the tips, giving it a most pleasing effect. The immense flowers are borne on long stiff but slender stems. The plant is a strong and sturdy grower and a free and continuous bloomer under all conditions, making it one of the most reliable for all purposes. Should be in every collection............ 1.00

**Special Offer—One root each of above 10 Colossal Cactus Dahlias, carefully labeled, by Parcel Post, prepaid, for $9.00.**

*QUEEN OF HEARTS. (See description opposite)*

# Select Standard Cactus Dahlias

The following embraces the very best standard Cactus varieties. We have grouped them as the best for general cultivation, from our observations in the fields. We offer them with the utmost confidence that they will give the greatest satisfaction to Dahlia lovers who want the very best in quantity. These varieties can be depended upon to give an abundance of bloom for all general purposes. For exhibitions we would refer to the **New and Rare** and **Colossal**, cactus varieties.

**Aegir.** Bright vermilion crimson. Petals beautifully Each twisted and whorled................ $0.25

**Amos Perry.** Brightest vermilion scarlet. Dwarf, very free bloomer. A fine garden variety............... .25

**Beauport Beauty.** Buff, suffused amber, very fine...... .25

**CANDEUR.** Large white, a strong vigorous grower, and an early and profuse bloomer. Long stiff stems...·.... .50

**Charm.** Yellow, shaded darker, tipped white.......... .25

**COMRADE.** A very pleasing variety of dwarf branching habit, producing the clear salmon pink flowers freely on stiff stems well above the foliage.................... .20

**Countess of Malmesbury.** Soft delicate pink with long quilled petals........................ .20

**Dainty.** Yellow, shaded salmon, suffused and overlaid pink........................ .25

**Elsa.** White, suffused yellow, overlaid pink and edged carmine rose. Very effective and pleasing............ .25

**Fairy Queen.** A beautiful garden variety. A pure white Each cactus of beautiful form, very long, narrow quilled incurved petals. The plant is medium dwarf and an extremely profuse bloomer................ $0.25

**Faunus.** Yellow, shading to rosy scarlet, long pointed petals. A beautiful flower........................ .25

**General Buller.** Very bold and striking. Rich velvety maroon, shading to crimson, tipped white; a profuse bloomer on stiff stems, well above the foliage......... .20

**Goliath.** Yellow, suffused and shaded orange salmon, fine form with good stems........................ .20

**Iolanthe.** Very large, long quilled incurved petals. Deep coral red, tipped gold. A strong vigorous grower with long slender graceful stem........................ .35

**J. B. Briant.** Very large, soft yellow, a fine exhibition variety; petals long, narrow and incurved........... .40

**J. H. JACKSON.** Still one of the best and most reliable of the so called black Dahlias; rich velvety maroon, shaded black. A fine large flower and a free bloomer.... .30

**KRIEMHILDE.** Deep cerise pink, tinting to creamy pink at centre. A distinct and valuable variety as the flowers keep a long time after cutting............... .25

**LAWINE.** A magnificent flower on long stems. A large white, lightly suffused pink. A strong vigorous grower, early and profuse bloomer. One of the best for commercial cut flowers and for the garden............ .25

**LIBELLE.** Another grand variety of medium size, a profuse bloomer on long stiff stems. Color a beautiful aster purple; very effective........................ .25

**Lyric.** Large rich yellow, shaded bronzy red. Plant is dwarf and an early and extremely profuse bloomer..... .50

**MARJORIE CASTLETON.** The best standard pink Cactus Dahlia. It is much softer than most of the pinks, and is an early, continuous bloomer. The color is soft rosy pink, tinting lighter toward the centre. It is a very rapid grower, with good stems and keeps well after cutting. (See illustration Page 5.).................... .25

**Mont Blanc Cactus.** Pure white and very finely formed, with long pointed incurved petals. A fine late bloomer, being full at the centre until frost. Never shows a yellow centre........................ .40

**Morning Glow.** Soft golden yellow, tipped bronzy amber. Large, fine form and profuse................ .50

**Mrs. Chas. Scott.** A fine bronzy yellow; large, finely formed, and a profuse bloomer. Always full at centre.. .35

**MRS. REGINALD BAILEY.** Large size, splendid form with long narrow incurved petals, always full centre. Color brilliant carmine crimson. A good bloomer on long stems........................ .50

**Perlehilde.** A delicate shell pink sport of Kriemhilde.... .20

**Pink Pearl.** Bright rose pink, tipped white; fine form, an early and profuse bloomer........................ .25

**QUEEN OF HEARTS.** A beautiful pure white with yellow at base of petals, making it a most lovely and effective flower. (See illustration opposite.).......... .25

**REINE CAYEUX.** Rich glowing cardinal red. An early and extremely profuse bloomer, with good stems. A grand garden and cut flower variety.....·........... .35

**Reliable.** Very large and profuse; salmon yellow, shaded darker........................ .40

**Rheinkoenig.** A large and very early profuse blooming white cactus........................ .25

**SEQUOIA.** Large golden bronze, fine form, long stiff stems. A strong grower and profuse bloomer. One of the best. .35

**The Pilot.** Yellow, heavily tipped bright terra cotta, very profuse........................ .25

**T. G. BAKER.** Very large, finely formed flowers on long stiff stems. One of the best........................ .35

**Uncle Tom.** Very dark rich maroon, shaded black, a free bloomer on long stiff stems.................... .25

**White Swan Cactus.** A beautiful pure white cactus, medium size and a profuse bloomer on long stiff stems. Fine for cutting and the garden.................... .25

**Special Offer—One each of the 36 Selected Standard Cactus Dahlias, strong roots, by Parcel Post, prepaid, for $10.00.**

**Cactus Dahlia Seed.** Seed from the best cactus Dahlias, all colors, mixed........................ $1.00

*One each, Bianca, Crystal, Mrs. Roosevelt, F. R. Austin, Radlyn and Gladys, 6 distinct types (see illustrations), for $3.00*

## Collarette Dahlias

A most uniquely distinct class or type, that has become quite popular. Every collection should include one or more of them. The flowers are single with a smaller row of small or collar petals. These collar petals are generally distinct in color from the outer row.

The accompanying illustration will give a general idea of the type. We know these will please you and add to the attractiveness of your collection.

|  | Each |
|---|---|
| **Albert Maumene.** Velvety crimson purple, margined white, collarette white | $0.25 |
| **ALTRO.** One of the most striking new collarettes, a wonderful and effective color combination. Rich crimson shaded maroon, margined and tipped white; collar petals white, slightly flushed crimson. New and distinct. | .50 |
| **ARDEN.** Very rich and effective deep golden yellow, blotched vivid orange crimson, collar pure yellow | .50 |
| **Compte. Chermeteff.** Cream suffused red, light collar | .25 |
| **DIAMENT.** Very large, velvety violet, collar light rose, very distinct and effective | .25 |
| **Dorian.** Rich crimson, shaded maroon; collar white suffused crimson | .50 |
| **ELGRAVE.** Duplex collarette, most novel and effective, with two or more rows of petals; rich maroon, collar petals maroon, heavily tipped white | .25 |
| **FAYETTE.** Another duplex collarette, bright scarlet with light yellow collar petals at base of each petal. The plant is a strong vigorous grower and free bloomer. Fine for garden or cutting, very striking and effective | .25 |
| **Henri Farman.** Yellow blotched red; cream collar, very pretty | .25 |
| **MARLEY.** Clear light canary yellow; a fine variety for cutting; very effective | .25 |
| **MAURICE REVOIRE.** Rich crimson maroon, white collar. Plant is a strong vigorous grower and profuse bloomer. Very effective | .25 |
| **Mrs. F. G. Bruant.** Very large, rich velvety maroon, with white collar; rich and striking | .25 |
| **Princess Louise.** An exquisite new variety; large; carmine and white; collar white suffused carmine | .25 |
| **RADLYN.** A beautiful variety; clear soft pink, collar same color (see light flower in illustration), very strong grower and free bloomer on long stiff stems, fine for cutting | .50 |

**Special Offer—One root of each of the 14 Select Collarette Dahlias described above for $3.25.**

**Seed.** Collarette Dahlia seed from above and other new varieties, all colors, per packet ..... $0.25

# New and Superb Decorative Dahlias
This is a remarkable collection of the World's Best Decoratives.

|  | Each |
|---|---|
| **AYESHA.** Immense size, clear light yellow, of beautiful regular form. The plant is a very strong vigorous grower and free bloomer. Fine for garden, exhibition and commercial purposes | $0.50 |
| **Beloit.** Immense size, the rich crimson flowers are of beautiful semi-cactus form and borne on long stiff stems. One of the very best Dahlias | 1.00 |
| **BLOEMHOVE.** Another immense flower that attracted attention. Similar in form to Bertha Van Suttner, but a beautiful clear lilac rose color. The plant is a sturdy and extremely profuse bloomer. The form is beautifully irregular with long reflex petals, resembling a huge broad leaved, reflexed chrysanthemum | 1.00 |
| **Berch von Heemstede.** Pure yellow, suffused a golden bronze; petals beautifully twisted and whorled, large and fine | 1.00 |
| **BREAK O'DAY.** A new giant flowered Dahlia that should be in every collection. Its immense size is relieved by a beautiful irregular formation and its soft color. A delicate clear sulphur yellow, tinting to sulphur white at the tips. The petals are of great substance, illuminated by a satiny sheen, giving the flowers a waxy appearance. A strong vigorous grower and free bloomer with long erect stems. An acquisition | 1.00 |
| **Challenge.** A very striking new decorative. Flowers large, yellow at the base, shading to bronzy red, tipped rich velvety oriental red. A fine grower and a good bloomer | 1.00 |
| **CHAS. LAWRENCE.** See description, Page 2 | $10.00 |
| **CHIEFTAIN.** Clear light red, heavily streaked and splashed canary yellow; some flowers all red; very large and attractive | 1.00 |
| **FANTASIE.** A new acquisition that promises to become a universal favorite. The flowers are very large, exquisite form and coloring. The color is entirely new and distinct, being salmon shaded blue. It is a very profuse bloomer | 1.50 |
| **Fireburst.** A massive flower, soft orange red, a free bloomer for garden or exhibition | .50 |
| **Glorie Lyonaise.** Very large, yellow suffused and tipped scarlet, profuse bloomer | 1.00 |
| **GOLDEN WEST DECORATIVE.** A big clear yellow decorative of close formation, with cleft petals. A strong vigorous grower and a free bloomer, producing the flowers on long erect stems. One of the finest for exhibition, cutting and the garden | .50 |
| **GOLDMINE.** The ideal pure golden yellow decorative Dahlia. Large, perfect form, with full high centre and a profuse bloomer on stiff stems. Very early | .50 |
| **Harmony.** Color very similar to Wodan; mauve rose with golden suffusion, good form and habit of growth | .50 |

*12 Beautiful Cactus Dahlias (our selection of varieties), all different and distinct, each labeled, $2.00*

*Decorative Dahlia, "JOHN WANAMAKER." (See description below)*

**HELEN DURNBAUGH.** A wonderful new mauve pink, of largest size and great substance. The plant is a strong vigorous grower and free bloomer on long stiff stems. One of the very best.......................... Each $2.00

**Herr Hohenzollern.** It is a new variety that will be grown universally as soon as the large, dark velvety red flowers are seen.................................. 1.00

**HORTULANUS FIET.** One of the loveliest Dahlias that ever came from Holland. The color is a creamy-salmon, shading to soft yellow. The flowers are large, and the formation and stems are both excellent. Free flowering........................................ .75

**HORTULANUS WITTE.** Very large, pure white; with good stems, one of the best....................... .50

**JANE SELBY.** One of the largest of all Dahlias. A delicate mauve pink of great substance and beautiful formation. The plant is a strong grower, producing the giant flowers on long stiff stems well above the foliage. A great acquisition and a flower that should be in every collection.................................... 1.50

### WHAT OTHERS SAY.

**JOHN WANAMAKER.** (See illustration.) One of the most beautifully formed of all Dahlias, large size, clear orchid pink, and an extremely early and profuse bloomer. **Awarded First Prize, Best Pink of any Class at the American Dahlia Society Exhibition in New York.** Each $0.50

**KATHERINE DE LA MARE.** See description, Page 2.. 2.00

**KING ALBERT.** In this we have a magnificently royal flower. Large, finely formed, rich royal purple. It is a strong vigorous grower and free bloomer........... 2.00

**KITTY DE LA MARE.** See description, Page 2....... 2.00

**Le Armour.** A lovely rich clear rosy cerise. White at base of petals; fine form and free bloomer. Stiff stems...... .50

**L. KRAMER PEACOCK.** The ideal white decorative for garden or cutting. The flowers are large, of perfect form, pure white and of great substance, keeping a long time after being cut. The plant is a strong vigorous grower of dwarf branching habit, a quick free grower and profuse bloomer........................................ .50

**Loveliness.** A fine large decorative, color soft mauve pink. .35

**Marianne.** Very large, rich crimson purple, tipped white, sometimes solid color, perfect form and a good bloomer. .50

**MARY STEFFENSON.** See description, Page 2....... 10.00

*Attraction, Golden West Cactus, General Pershing, Kalif Nibelungenhort and Yellow King, 6 wonderful Hybrid Cactus Giants, $4.00*

*Decorative Dahlia, "MINNIE BURGLE." (See description below)*

**MINNIE BURGLE.** One of the best, rich cardinal red of fine form and produced freely on long stiff stems. Plant is a strong vigorous upright grower and profuse bloomer. (See illustration above)........................ **Each** $0.50

**MME. MARZE.** Immense pure white, the giant flowers are produced freely on long stiff stems.............. .50

**Mme. Victor Vassier.** Very large, clear soft yellow, of fine decorative form. A fine plant and a free bloomer... .50

**MRS. C. H. BRECK.** One of the most effective varieties for all purposes. Color soft yellow, suffused and tipped carmine, bright and effective. The plant is a strong vigorous grower of dwarf branching habit and an early, profuse and continuous bloomer. The flowers are large and borne on stiff erect stems. It is a hybrid decorative. .50

**MRS. THOS. BUSH.** A fine new variety. Color reddish salmon, tinting to primrose yellow at centre and tipped rose; of immense size on long stems................. 1.50

**NANCY ALDEN.** See description, Page 2............. 1.00

**PATRICK O'MARA.** See description, Page 2. Strong plants.......................................... 10.00

**PRINCE OF ORANGE.** A giant flower, 7 to 9 inches across, rich orange, shaded scarlet. The flowers are produced on magnificent cane stiff stems, 3 feet long and borne erect. A wonderful exhibition flower.......... 1.00

**Pink Flamingo.** An early bloomer, of large size and fine form, sometimes showing an open centre. Color violet rose, overlaid tyrian rose; very free flowering........ **Each** $0.50

**QUEEN MARY.** A grand decorative that has proven its worth as the best deep pink for all purposes. The size is large to very large, full high centre, even up to November 10th, 1920, when killed by frost. Color clear silvery cerise pink. The plant is a strong healthy vigorous upright branching grower, producing the giant flowers freely on long stiff stems. (See illustration, page 10).. .50

**ROBERT SHEPPARD.** See description, Page 2....... 1.00

**Sunlight.** A fine yellow, suffused bronze, very large on stiff stems........................................ 1.00

**SYLVANIA.** One of the very finest of large size, fine form and a free bloomer on long stiff stems. Color soft lilac pink, tinting lighter toward centre............... 2.00

**Special Offer.** We will send one root each of the 41 New and Superb Decorative Dahlias listed above for $58.00; without Charles Lawrence, Katherine de La Mare, Kitty de la Mare, Mary Steffenson, Nancy Alden, Patrick O'Mara and Robert Sheppard, a superb collection of 34 of the World's Best Decoratives for $27.00.

**Seed.** Decorative Dahlia seed from best named varieties, all colors, per packet, $1.00.

*Mrs. C. H. Breck, L. Kramer Peacock, Ayesha, Queen Mary, Dr. Tyrrel and Minnie Burgle, 6 World's Best Decoratives, $2.00*

*Decorative Dahlia, "QUEEN MARY." (See description, page 9)*

# Select Decorative Dahlias

Selected from the best standard varieties. All are good bloomers and will give the greatest satisfaction.

**A. C. Ide.** Very large, rich velvety maroon; a fine garden and exhibition variety; an early and free bloomer..... $0.50

**American Beauty.** Deep red, very large. A massive flower................................................. .50

**CRIMSON GIANT.** Richest glowing red; very large size, and a very strong, vigorous grower ............. .25

**CUBAN GIANT.** Very large; deep crimson shaded maroon, fine form, long stems...................... .25

**DELICE.** The best pure bright rose pink, entirely distinct, beautiful form............................... .30

**DR. TYRREL.** (See illustration, Page 11.) A very large, rich bronzy golden yellow, shaded orange. A rather late flower of great size, on long stiff stems............... .30

**Flora.** A large, pure white decorative. A strong grower and profuse bloomer on long stems................. .25

**GEN'L J. B. SETH.** Very large and perfectly formed with rather broad petals; color a rich strawberry red. An early and profuse bloomer...................... $0.35

**GRAND DUKE ALEXIS.** Very large flower with quilled petals. Color white, lightly edged lavender pink. A strong grower and free bloomer. One of the best...... .50

**Henry Patrick.** Large snow white flowers, beautiful form and great substance......................... .25

**JACK ROSE.** The best crimson for garden or cutting; that brilliant crimson red that made the "Jack" Rose popular and suggested the name.................... .25

**Jan Olieslager.** Very large, pure yellow............. .75

**Jumbo.** Deep red, shaded maroon, very free.......... .25

**LE GRAND MANITOU.** Immense size; lilac penciled crimson, extra fine; dwarf......................... .75

*Grand Duke Alexis, Red Duke, Yellow Duke, Mme. Marze, Prof. Mansfield and Break O'Day. A fine set of 6 Giants for $2.00*

*Decorative Dahlia, "DR. TYRREL." (See description, page 10)*

**Lord Penn.** Large purple with quilled petals, an early and profuse bloomer......................................... **Each $0.25**

**LYNDHURST.** Brightest vermilion; the best bright red for cutting. An early, free and continuous bloomer on long straight stems.......................................... .25

**MELODY.** One of the finest, being of splendid regular form with full high centre and reflexed outer petals. Color clear canary yellow, tinting to creamy white at the tips; an effect so delicate and pleasing as to suggest the name............................................................ .25

**MINNIE McCULLOUGH.** (See illustration, Page 13.) One of the most indispensable decorative varieties that is largely, but should be universally, grown. It is entirely distinct, in a class by itself, on account of the combination of Autumn shades—the gold and red of Autumn leaves. The illustration shows the form and average size, but the flowers must be seen to be fully appreciated. Especially under artificial light. Selected stock............................................................ .25

**MME. A. LUMIERE.** One of the most distinct and pleasing. A wonderfully attractive and effective color combination; white, tipped bright violet red. A fine plant of branching habit, producing the bright perfect formed medium size flowers in greatest profusion on stiff stems.......................................... .50

**MONT BLANC.** A splendid large white of beautiful form and great substance, produced freely on long stiff stems............................................................ **Each $0.50**

**Mrs. Chas. Turner.** Very large, pure yellow.......... .30

**Mrs. J. Gardner Cassatt.** Bright cerise pink, large flowers on long stiff stems............................ .25

**MRS. ROOSEVELT.** We are glad to announce we again have a fine stock of this grand decorative. (See illustration, Page 12.) The flowers are of giant size and borne on long stems. Color a lovely shade of enchantress pink. The plant is a strong vigorous grower.......... .50

**Oregon Beauty.** Very bright vermilion cardinal, rich and glistening, flowers are large on long graceful stems...... .35

**PERLE DE LYON.** Splendid pure white. Similar to Perle de 'Or, but better............................ .35

**Perle de Parc.** Very large white with long stiff stems. A profuse bloomer.................................. .25

**PINK JACK ROSE.** A pink sport of Jack Rose; a very free bloomer and fine for bedding.................... .25

**Princess Juliana.** A fine pure white of good size on long cane stiff stems; very profuse...................... .50

*12 Best Standard Decoratives, all distinct and named. Our selection of varieties, $2.00*

*Decorative Dahlia, "MRS. ROOSEVELT." (See description, page 11)*

**PROFESSOR MANSFIELD.** A giant decorative of most unique coloring; a pleasing combination of yellow, red and white.................................................. $0.25

**Progress.** Large mauve, striped and penciled crimson... .25

**Propoganda.** Primrose yellow, lightly suffused crimson on reverse of petals.............................. .25

**RED DUKE.** Very large, rich dazzling cardinal red; splendid form with quilled petals. A red Grand Duke Alexis.......................................... .25

**Souvenir de Gustav Doazon.** One of the largest of all Dahlias, soft orange red.......................... .25

**SYLVIA.** Deep pink, tinting to light pink at the centre; large perfectly formed flowers produced profusely on long stiff stems. This variety is indispensable where quantity of flowers are wanted. It is a strong vigorous grower, and always blooms Selected stock............ .25

**Wm. Agnew.** Bright fiery scarlet, flowers large on long stiff graceful stems; fine for the garden............... .25

**YELLOW DUKE.** Canary yellow, quilled petals; a giant flower on long stems............................ .25

**Special Offer—One root each of the 36 selected Standard Decorative Dahlias described above, by Parcel Post, prepaid, for $10.00.**

## What Others Say

### The "F. R. Austin" Blooms Continually.

BUFFALO, N. Y., November 10th, 1920.

PEACOCK DAHLIA FARMS, INC., Berlin, N. J.

GENTLEMEN:—Early last Spring I ordered from you a selection of dahlias and also purchased your Dahlia Book, and followed instructions accordingly. I am simply writing to advise you that I have had very satisfactory results. I cut the first bloom of the "F. R. Austin" July 10th, and the last one on October 15th. It bloomed continuously. In fact all that you sent me were continuously in bloom and I still have a few blooms in the house at this date. I have had them as large as 7¼ inches in diameter, and they were admired by a great many people.

Although I have not very much space I shall order a few more varieties next Spring.

Very truly yours, H. F. KEITSCH.

### "The Dahlia"—The Only Thorough Book.

OKLAHOMA CITY, OKLAHOMA.

PEACOCK DAHLIA FARMS, Berlin, N. J.

MY DEAR MR. PEACOCK:—"The Dahlia" fifth edition arrived and has been read from cover to cover and to say I am charmed with it puts it mildly. It is the only really thorough book on Dahlia Culture that I have been able to get. Thank you very much. The dahlias from you are coming up nicely.

MRS. A. L. FORTÈ, Rural Route No. 9.

*Jack Rose, Lyndhurst, Sylvia, Melody, Queen of Hearts, White Swan, Minnie McCullough, Albert Maumene, Marjorie Castleton, Maurice Revoir, Klein Domitea and Mrs. Jos. Lucas, 12 fine Dahlias, for $2.00*

*Paeony Dahlia, "F. R. AUSTIN." (See description below)*

## Paeony Flowered Dahlias

This is one of the newer types also called the Art or Artistic Dahlias. The true type resembles the Japanese Paeony; yet several of the most valuable and popular varieties differ from the true type.

**AUTUMN GLOW.** A most distinct and striking autumn shade. The outer petals are deep pinkish scarlet, with yellow markings and tip, and each row of petals opens up softer against the darker background of the outer petals. A strong grower producing the large flowers freely on long stiff stems.................................... $1.50

**BARON G. DE GRANCY.** A waxy, almost pure white; a flower of excellent type, perfect form and purity of color. The blooms are borne profusely on long graceful stems.......................................................... .30

**BERNICE.** Soft rose pink, very broad petals, very large flowers on stiff slender stems.................................... .50

**BILLIE.** Color light rose, tipped violet rose with a suggestion of yellow at the base of the petals, the general effect being a bright rose pink. Flowers are of beautiful form with petals curved and twisted, averaging at least six inches across on long stems............................ 1.00

**BRILLIANTINE.** A medium to small variety that is without doubt the richest and highest colored of all Dahlias. White shading to carmine, tipped glowing cardinal carmine. A wonderful bloomer and fine for cutting and the garden........................................ $0.75

**CANARY.** Pure canary yellow of very largest size; an early, free and continuous bloomer on long slender stems, one of the best........................................................ .30

**F. R. AUSTIN.** (See illustration above.) One of the most striking and valuable paeony Dahlias in existence. The beautifully colored flowers are of large size, averaging 6 to 8 inches across, while the illustration shown above shows its fine form. Color, the outer petals are very long, creamy yellow, suffused, banded and shaded rich crimson; the inner petals are yellow at base tinting lighter, and suffused pink and crimson. The plant is a strong vigorous grower, an extremely early and free bloomer, and continues to bloom the entire season, making it most valuable for garden and exhibition.... .50

**SPECIAL OFFER.** 6 wonderful Giant Century Dahlias: Cream Century, Geisha Century, Mrs. Wendel Reber, Mrs. Jos. Lucas, Rose Pink and Yellow Century for $1.00

13

**DELICATINE.** An exquisitely beautiful new paeony; white suffused pink, overlaid and shaded crimson. Plant is dwarf, branching, a profuse bloomer on stiff slender stems.... **$2.00** (Each)

**Dr. Peary.** Very large deep crimson, shaded maroon, the best of its class .............. .50

**FORDHOOK BEAUTY.** An outstanding shade of bronzy red, delicately suffused with salmon and yellow. A beauty ................... .50

**GEISHA.** The most striking color combination, golden yellow, changing to bright scarlet at the center of petal and back to gold at the tip. Giant flowers on long wiry stems...... 1.00

**Hortulanus Budde.** Large rich scarlet on long stems. A strong grower and free bloomer.... .35

**JESSIE CAIN.** Golden yellow at base of petals, suffused and blotched scarlet, tipped yellow. A beautiful flower of large size with broad, slightly pointed, petals................... 1.00

**Konigen Emma.** Very large cerise pink...... .35

**Mme. Van Loon.** Soft orange scarlet, large and free................................ .35

**MRS. G. GORDON.** A beautiful large primrose yellow, shading to light yellow, fine form. A profuse bloomer...................... .50

**MRS. HOWARD M. EARL.** An exquisitely lovely paeony, light yellow, suffused and overlaid carmine scarlet, tipped yellow. A refined and glorified Geisha. Plant is very strong, producing the flowers on long graceful stems. Owing to the great demand, stock is very limited.................... **$2.00** (Each)

**Mrs. Robert Bates.** Pink white on long stiff stems. An early and profuse bloomer...................... .50

**Poinsettia.** Very bright and effective. Brilliant scarlet with long broad, but pointed, petals like the poinsettia.. .50

**QUEEN ELIZABETH.** See description, Page 1........ 1.00

**Rankin.** Large light lemon yellow................... .50

**RUFFLES.** A new sensation that attracted attention the past season. It is a giant ruffled paeony collarette. Red veined and tipped light bronzy yellow. The collar petals are light yellow, making it most effective, a profuse bloomer. In addition to the ruffled flowers, the leaves are also ruffled. It is a strong vigorous grower and bears the giant flowers most gracefully.............. 1.50

**Thos. Walkins.** Flowers are large, of beautiful form and coloring. White suffused cerise, heavily shaded and tipped crimson.................................... 1.00

**TYRREL AUSTIN.** See description, Page 2.......... 3.00

**Sensation.** Bright scarlet, heavily tipped white. Plant a very strong vigorous grower and profuse bloomer on long stiff stems.................................... .50

**UNIQUE.** This is not only unique in coloring, but in form, Half of the flowers are perfectly full to the centre, of fine regular form; the other half of them have numerous curled and twisted petals, almost covering the centre and other fantastic forms. Color is rich rosy mauve, with crimson shade at base of petal, very striking and effective 1.00

**VARIEGATED LISTZ.** Dark oriental red with yellow tips and markings. A superior variety for decorations, especially where a bronzy effect is wanted.............. .25

**WM. AUSTIN.** A strong vigorous plant that comes into bloom early and continues until frost. Flowers large, finely formed; color white, suffused cerise, tipped carmine; very long stiff stems...................... 1.00

**Special Offer—One root each of the above 28 Superb Paeony Dahlias by Parcel Post, prepaid for $20.00.**

**Seed.** Paeony Dahlia seed from best varieties, all colors, per packet..................................... .50

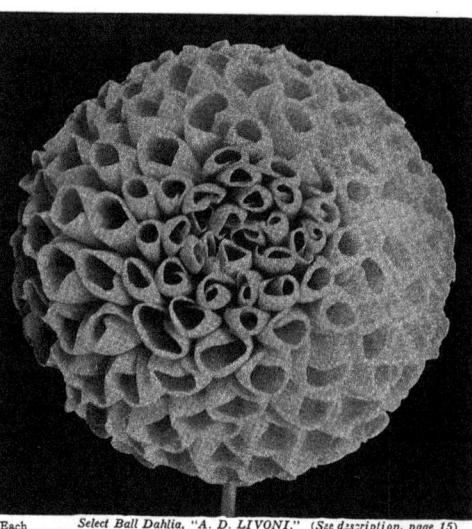

*Select Ball Dahlia, "A. D. LIVONI." (See description, page 15)*

# New and Rare Ball Dahlias

This is a superb collection that attracted the greatest attention from thousands of visitors on account of the distinct coloring, large size and long stems.

**Arthur Le Favour.** Very large yellow penciled and striped cardinal red.................................. **$0.50** (Each)

**AUGUS MEGAR.** A very fine lavender purple. Large fine form and borne on long stiff stems.............. .75

**Della Dorsheimer.** Large, soft shrimp pink, quilled petals; long slender stems........................... .30

**DOROTHY DE LA MARE.** A magnificent new variety of the most delicate pink color, perfect ball form, the outer petals reflexing to the stem. The plant is a strong, heavy and vigorous grower, producing the giant flowers on long stiff graceful stems. An early, free and continuous bloomer................................ 3.00

**Dreers White.** Very large, pure white, quilled petals. A dwarf grower with long drooping stems. A good bloomer .50

**DREERS YELLOW.** A very fine, rich yellow of largest size; quilled petals. Always full to the centre. A strong, vigorous grower and free bloomer on long stiff stems.... .50

**ELECTRIC SHOW.** Large, full ball type, color a soft magenta rose, very fine............................ .50

**Elsa Burgess.** Large, white suffused and tipped lavender. .25

**IVANHOE.** Very large, white suffused and edged soft lavender pink.................................... .50

**MERLIN.** Bright red, beautiful form, a dwarf grower, early and profuse bloomer...................... .50

**MISS HELEN HOLLIS.** Very large, rich vermilion scarlet of beautiful form and always full to the centre. A tall strong vigorous grower and a free bloomer...... 1.00

**Mme. Alfred Moreau.** Very large, light cerise pink. A fine grower with long stiff stems..................... .50

**MME. H. FURTADO.** A fine large pure white of fine form and a profuse bloomer on erect stems........... .50

**Mrs. Saunders.** Very large yellow, tipped white........ .50

**MRS. THOS. SHARP.** This is one of the most exquisite in coloring and habit. A rich golden orange of rather loose formation, but very regular and always full to the centre; medium to large size. The plant is a dwarf branching, spreading habit and an extremely profuse bloomer. Fine for garden or cutting................. 1.00

*The 10 New Introductions of 1921, described on pages 1 and 2, to those who want the best, for $40.00*

**Perfection.** Perfect form, yellow, suffused and tipped rose, long stiff stems.......................... $0.50

**ROSE.** An exquisite Ball Dahlia of full regular form and a bright lively carmine rose color; it is very distinct, large flowers on long stiff stems..................... .50

**STRADELLA.** Deep purple crimson, early and profuse.. .50

**W. W. RAWSON.** Very large with semi-quilled petals. Long upright stems, color white, delicately flushed and suffused lilac..................................... .50

Special Offer—One root each of the 19 New and Rare Ball Dahlias, by Parcel Post, prepaid, for $10.00.

**Seed.** We have a limited quantity of Ball Dahlia seed from best varieties, all colors, per packet............. 1.00

## Select Ball Dahlias

**A. D. LIVONI.** Clear cerise pink, quilled petals. A free bloomer and a great favorite (see description, page 14). $0.20

**Apolyon.** Brightest scarlet.......................... .20

**Aurora.** Yellow suffused and tipped orange........... .25

**Bonton.** Medium size, rich crimson, shaded darker. A free bloomer of large size on long stems.............. .25

**CAROL.** A beautiful ball of small size, but beautiful round full form, with quilled petals and clear pink color. Large strong plants and produces the lovely flowers freely on long stiff stems............................ .50

**Crimson Globe.** Bright crimson. A profuse bloomer... .25

**DOROTHY PEACOCK.** The world's best pink........ .50

**Duchess of York.** Yellow heavily tipped carmine, shaded darker. A fine variety............................. .25

**Emily May.** Yellow suffused bronzy red............. .25

**METEOR.** Large, bright vermilion, a free bloomer...... .35

**Penelope.** White flaked rosy lake, beautiful effect...... .25

**Pink Swan.** A silvery pink sport of White Swan......... .25

**Princess Victoria.** Small clear light yellow, profuse bloomer................................................ .25

**Queen Victoria.** Rich golden yellow, quilled petals. A strong grower and a profuse bloomer................. .25

**RED HUSSAR.** Richest dazzling cardinal red. A strong vigorous grower and a free bloomer on long stems. Best red show Dahlia for cutting...................... .25

**Susan.** Soft blush pink, medium size. Good form...... .30

**TANSBORO.** Crimson shaded maroon, white suffused crimson at base of petals, early and profuse........... .50

**Tom Watson.** Large, creamy white, quilled petals...... .25

**WHITE SWAN.** Pure white, the standard commercial white Ball Dahlia. A strong grower and free bloomer... .20

Special Offer—One each of the above 19 Select Ball Dahlias by Parcel Post, prepaid, for $4.50.

## Pompon Dahlias

This class is a miniature form of the show and fancy Dahlias, having the same round, ball like form, but much smaller in size. The plants are also smaller, of branching habit, producing the flowers in endless profusion. As they can be cut in sprays they are valuable for bouquets and for small grounds.

Each

**Allie Mourey.** Light pink, tipped deep pink........... $0.25

**Bobby.** Plum color; very fine; free flowering sort...... .25

**Clara Harsh.** Yellow tipped crimson. Very pretty...... .50

***CLARISSA.** Pale primrose. A free bloomer.......... .25

***ELEGANTA.** Very pretty, light pink, suffused and tipped deep pink. Quilled petals.................... .25

**Elfin.** Very small and dainty. Light primrose yellow.... .25

***KLEIN DOMITEA.** Bright golden terra-cotta. Profuse.................................................. .25

***LITTLE HERMAN.** Cardinal red, shaded maroon, tipped white.......................................... .25

**Little Sweetheart.** Red, tipped white................. .25

**Madeline.** Primrose, edged rosy purple............... .25

***SNOWCLAD.** The best pure white pompon.......... .25

**Sunshine.** Brightest vermilion, beautiful regular form on long stems..................................... .25

Special Offer—One root each of the 5 Pompon Dahlias marked with an asterisk (*), by Parcel Post, prepaid, for $1.00.

**Seed.** Pompon Dahlia seed from best varieties, all colors, per packet............................................ .50

## Best Single Dahlias

The ordinary single Dahlias have been superseded by the Century Dahlias, but a few of the most beautiful or distinctive are appreciated, especially where color effects, smaller flowers or dwarf plants are needed.

Each

**AMI BARILLET.** The purple foliage Dahlia. Entirely distinct. Flowers pure garnet, rich and glowing with a dark center, until the pollen appears. A free bloomer and strikingly effective for all purposes............. $0.50

**APPLE BLOSSOMS.** Soft pink, heavily tipped carmine pink edged crimson, changing to softer tints as the season advances................................................ .25

**FLORABUNDA.** Very free, mauve, with red zone around yellow center....................................... .25

**HAZEL HEITER.** A high colored single, a fine combination of pink, crimson and maroon.................... .25

**PRAXITELLES.** The color is a deep velvety violet maroon, each petal tipped white. The plants are dwarf, branching and profuse bloomers; the colors distinct and striking. This is undoubtedly the richest, the most popular and most effective of all fancy Single Dahlias.. .25

**RANTENDELIN.** Another fancy single. Color pure white, each petal has a narrow margin of deep crimson on each side. A very profuse bloomer. Plant dwarf and branching. Height, 3 feet........................... .25

**ST. GEORGE.** Clear canary yellow, a splendid plant, branching, very profuse on long slender stems........ .25

Special Offer—One root each of the 7 Best Single Dahlias, by Parcel Post, prepaid, for $1.50.

## Superb Century Dahlias

**Anna Long.** Clear rosy pink, with white band running through each petal; sometimes solid pink........... $0.25

**CREAM CENTURY.** Delicate creamy white, beautiful form on long stems............................... .20

**ECKFORD CENTURY.** Immense flower, white centered pink, spotted and penciled crimson. Free bloomer on long stems........................................... .25

**EVELYN CENTURY.** Very bright and striking, white, outer half of petals a bright violet cerise making a beautiful white zone around the yellow disc............... .35

**GEISHA CENTURY.** Yellow and scarlet, very bright and attractive; strong grower with long stiff stems.... .25

**JOSEPHINE.** Large pure white, free bloomer, stiff stems, very fine................................... .50

**Josie.** A fine white, very free...................... .25

**MRS. JOSEPH LUCAS.** A combination of autumn shades. Immense size, beautiful form, produced profusely on good stiff stems. Yellow suffused orange and overlaid salmon pink. One of the largest and handsomest................................................ .50

**MRS. WENDEL REBER.** Another giant flower, buff yellow, suffused and overlaid orange scarlet. A strong vigorous grower; long stiff stems.................... .25

**ROSE PINK CENTURY.** The largest and best deep pink; enormous flowers on long three feet stems; a sure and continuous bloomer, vigorous plant.......... .25

**20th CENTURY.** The original century, originated and introduced by us in 1901. Early in the season color an intense rosy crimson shading to white at tips, and base of petals; but as the season advances the flowers open lighter until by October they are nearly white, a bright pink blotch in the centre of the petals............... .25

**WILDFIRE CENTURY.** Century size, with the brilliant, rich scarlet of the old Wildfire. Acknowledged the best commercial scarlet................................. .20

**YELLOW CENTURY.** A magnificent yellow of largest size, beautiful form and a profuse bloomer on long stiff stems............................................... .25

Special Offer—One root each of the above 13 Superb Century Dahlias by Parcel Post, prepaid, for $3.00.

*5 lovely Pompon Dahlias marked by asterisk for $1.00*

15

*"GIANT CENTURY." Reduced Size. (See description below)*

# New and Rare Century Dahlias

Are the last word in this popular type and we take great pleasure in introducing such a grand set, in such a wide range of colors, types and characteristics as embraced in the following collection.

**ALICE.** Pure white; very large and finely formed. A profuse bloomer on long stems ............... Each $0.50

**AUTUMN CENTURY.** A fine bronzy variety; large fine form on long stems. Color, buff yellow at base of petals shading through amber to red, with an iridescent sheen. .35

**BARTON.** Rich vivid crimson, large size, finest regular form and a profuse bloomer on long stems .......... .50

**BRONZE CENTURY.** A magnificent new century of immense size; rich bronzy yellow, produced profusely on long stiff stems. Splendid form and substance; especially effective under artificial light ................ .50

**CONTRAST.** Very large, crimson tipped white. Born on long stiff stems ............. .75

**GARNET CENTURY.** Rich glowing garnet, fine form, on long stems, a very profuse bloomer .......... .50

**GEORGE YOUNG.** A magnificent pure yellow of largest size. Long stiff but graceful stems ........... .50

**GLADYS CENTURY.** This new seedling is one of the most remarkable in coloring. A rich carmine band runs through the centre of the outer half of the petal, margined on either side with carmine pink; the inner half of each petal is white making a white zone around the yellow disc. Most striking and effective .......... .50

**GIANT CENTURY.** Immense size, finest form and beautiful color combination. Color is yellow at base, shading to bronzy salmon and crimson, with lighter tips. Undoubtedly the largest single Dahlia in existence, producing the giant blooms 7 to 10 inches across. See illustration above .............................. Each $1.50

**GLORIA.** Rich yellow, tipped and penciled vivid red; flowers of great substance, on long rigid stems. Very bright and effective .............................. .35

**JAMES WELLER.** (See description in new introductions, Page 2) .............................. 2.00

**JESSIE.** The greatest white single Dahlia in existence. Exquisite form, pure white, of large size and borne profusely on long slender but stiff stems ................ .50

**PURPLE CENTURY.** Rich royal purple, immense size; a most popular color, beautiful form .............. .50

**VELVET CENTURY.** Rich velvety maroon, very fine .. .50

**VERMILION CENTURY.** Brightest vermilion, very fine regular form, profuse bloomer on long stems ...... .50

**Special Offer—One root each of the 15 New and Rare Century Dahlias, a glorious collection of artistic beauties, by Parcel Post, prepaid, for $8.00.**

**Seed.** Seed from the best Century varieties, all colors, per packet .............................. .25

*NEW BOOK, "THE DAHLIA," FREE on request with orders amounting to $5.00 or more*

16

# *Join* THE AMERICAN DAHLIA SOCIETY

FORMED for the purpose of stimulating interest in and promoting the culture and development of the Dahlia; to establish a standard nomenclature; to test new varieties and to give them such recognition as they deserve; to study the diseases of the Dahlia and find remedies for same, and to disseminate information relating to this flower; to secure uniformity in awarding prizes at flower shows, and to give exhibitions when deemed advisable.

Dahlia growers, amateurs or professionals, are invited to exhibit at the Dahlia Show, Hotel Pennsylvania, New York, September 27, 28, 29 and 30, 1921. The entire roof garden and conservatory will be filled with Dahlias.

*Sample copy of Bulletin sent FREE*

FROM

Name ..............................

Town ..............................

State ..............................

# PEACOCK DAHLIA FARMS

## BERLIN POST OFFICE

## NEW JERSEY

# PEACOCK DAHLIA FARMS,

POST OFFICE ADDRESS
**Berlin, New Jersey**

*Date*............................................................................192......

Name, ....................................................................................................
 *Ladies will please put the prefix Miss or Mrs.*

Street Address or
Box Number ....................................................................................

Post Office, ...............................................................................

County, .........................................................................................

R. D. Route,..................... State,...............................................

**State here whether you want shipment
to be made by Mail, Express, or Freight.**

...........................................................................................................
*If different from Post Office give* }............................................................
*name of Express or Freight Office* }

AMOUNT ENCLOSED

Post Office Money Order, . . . . $..............................

Express Money Order, . . . . . $..............................

Draft or Check, . . . . . . . $..............................

Cash, . . . . . . . . . . $..............................

Stamps, . . . . . . . . . . $..............................

Total, . . . $..............................

*Please Leave This Space Blank*

| Quantity | NAME OF VARIETY | Price | Amount |
| --- | --- | --- | --- |

Decorative Dahlia, "MINNIE McCULLOUGH." (See description, page 11)

# WHAT OTHERS SAY

### Says Peacock's Bulbs are the Best Bulbs.

BRONX, N. Y., February 17, 1920.

PEACOCK DAHLIA FARMS, INC., Berlin, N. J.
DEAR SIRS:—I feel I owe the Peacock Dahlia Farms a few lines to show my appreciation for your valuable book "The Dahlia" which I received from you two years ago. For 18 years I have grown Dahlias for pleasure with a certain amount of success. But with the bulbs and book bought of you, I last year grew them to exhibition size, some 8 inches across with stems 26½ inches long. There is but one book "The Dahlia," and the best bulbs are from Peacock Dahlia Farms.

Very truly yours, JOHN BRANDUM.

### Was Successful for 30 Years.

OFFICE OF THE COUNTY TREASURER.
PITTSFIELD, MASS.

PEACOCK DAHLIA FARMS, Berlin, N. J.
GENTLEMEN:—The box containing the dahlias, which you sent me, received yesterday. I hasten to return thanks for your liberality in exceeding the number that I expected and for such promising roots.
I was led to begin the cultivation of dahlias from the purchase of Mr. Lawrence K. Peacock's first edition of his book "The Dahlia" some thirty years or more ago, and soon after the sending to him an order. Each season since I have continued with varying success.

Yours truly, HENRY A. BREWSTER.

### Likes our Methods of Doing Business.

THE PITTSBURG STOCK EXCHANGE.
OFFICE OF THE SECRETARY.
PITTSBURG, PENNA., May 19, 1920.

PEACOCK DAHLIA FARMS, INC., Berlin, N. J.
DEAR SIRS:—I beg to acknowledge receipt of the Dahlia Roots by Parcel Post, and wish to say it is a pleasure to do business with a house like you.

Very truly, C. J. HOLMAN.

### Thinks Our Farms Worth Visiting.

JENKINTOWN, PENNA., November 9th, 1920.

PEACOCK DAHLIA FARMS, Berlin, N. J.
GENTLEMEN:—Kindly send me catalogue of your dahlias. I visited your place November 7th. It is a most wonderful sight. I wish to order more bulbs to be sent along with order placed while at the farms.

Very truly, MRS. H. R. STOOPS.

### Californian Much Pleased with Our Stock

SANTA BARBA COUNTY HORTICULTURAL SOCIETY.
OFFICE OF THE SECRETARY.

PEACOCK DAHLIA FARMS, Berlin, N. J.
DEAR SIRS:—I gave you a small order last Spring for $10.00 worth of Dahlias. Your stock in O. K. I am much pleased with it.

Yours truly, W. J. TREDMARSH.

THE WORLD'S BEST DAHLIAS

ACTUAL SIZE
7 1/8 IN'S

Golden West
Cactus
SEE DESCRIPTION PAGE 1

PEACOCK DAHLIA FARMS

FARMS
WILLIAMSTOWN JUNCTION
NEW JERSEY

MAIL ADDRESS
BERLIN POST OFFICE
NEW JERSEY